ENGLISH FOLK-CHANTEYS

WITH PIANOFORTE ACCOMPANIMENT
INTRODUCTION AND
NOTES

COLLECTED BY

CECIL J. SHARP

London:

SIMPKIN, MARSHALL, HAMILTON, KENT & CO., LTD.

SCHOTT & CO., LTD.

Taunton: BARNICOTT & PEARCE, THE WESSEX PRESS

MCMXIV

PREFACE.

WISH *to express my gratitude to those who have so kindly and readily sung to me the songs recorded in the following pages; and to offer my thanks to the Rev. A. A. Brockington and Mr. Fleetwood Stileman for the valuable help which they have given me in the course of my investigations.*

C. J. S.

CONTENTS.

vii

Alphabetical Index of Chanteys.

INTRODUCTION.

HE sailors' chantey is, I imagine, the last of the labour-songs to survive in this country. In bygone days there must have been an enormous number of songs of this kind associated with every rhythmical form of manual labour ; but the machine killed the landsman's work-song too long ago for it now to be recoverable. The substitution, too, of the steam-engine for the sail in deep-sea craft has given the death-blow to the chantey ; but in this case there are, happily, many old sailors still living who can recall and are ready to sing the songs that they used to chant tramping round the capstan, or when yards were raised and sails hoisted or furled.

How old the chantey may be it is impossible to say, but that the custom amongst sailors of singing in rhythm with their work was in vogue as far back at least as the fifteenth century, the vivid description of the voyage in " The Complaynt of Scotland " (c. 1450) places beyond question.

Notwithstanding the antiquity of the chantey the word itself is quite modern ; indeed, the compilers of the Oxford Dictionary are unable to cite its use in literature earlier than 1869. Moreover, although the authorities are more or less in agreement regarding the derivation of the word (Fr. chanté), its spelling is still in dispute. The Oxford Dictionary (1913) gives the pre-ference to " shanty " ; Webster's New International Dictionary (1911) to " chantey " ; while the Century Dictionary (1889) prints both forms " chantey " and " shanty." Clark Russell and Kipling write it " chantey," and Henley " chanty." As the balance of expert opinion appears to favour " chantey " that spelling is adopted here.

Considering the interest which this subject must have for antiquaries, musicians, folk-lorists and others, its bibliography is remarkably slender. Of the Collections, containing both words and music, that have so far been published, the following must, I think, be regarded as the most important :—

Sailors' Songs or Chanties ; Davis and Tozer (1st ed., 1887).

Music of the Waters ; Laura Alexandrine Smith (1888).

Ships, Sea Songs and Shanties ; W. B. Whall (1st ed., 1910 ; 2nd ed., 1912).

Songs of Sea Labour (Chanties) ; Bullen and Arnold (1914).

Of these, the last two are at once the most recent and, in my opinion, the most authoritative. Each is the compilation of a professional sailor and avowedly a one-man collection, containing those chanteys only which its author had himself heard and learned at sea.

Here, of course, Mr. Whall and Mr. Bullen have the advantage of me. I have no technical or practical knowledge whatever of nautical matters ; I have never even heard a chantey sung on board ship. But then I approach the subject from its æsthetic side—my concern is solely with the music of the chantey and with its value as an art-product and this I contend is quite possible even for one who is as ignorant as I am of the technical details of the subject.

Counting variants, I have collected upwards of 150 chanteys, all of which have been taken down from the lips of old sailors now living in retirement at St. Ives, Padstow, Watchet, Bridgwater, Clevedon, Bristol, Newcastle and London. In making my selection for the purposes of this book I have been guided by the following considerations. I have limited my choice to those chanteys which I had definite evidence were actually used within living memory as working-songs on board ship ; I have excluded every example of the sea-song or ballad, which is, of course, not a labour-song at all ; I have omitted certain popular and undoubtedly genuine chanteys, such as " The Banks of the Sacramento," " Poor Paddy works on the Railway," " Can't you dance the Polka," " Good-bye, Fare you Well," etc.,—all of which are included, I believe, in one or other of the Collections above enumerated—on the ground that the tunes are not of folk-origin, but rather the latter-day adaptations of popular, " composed " songs of small musical value ; and finally, to save space, I have excluded several well-known chanteys, *e.g.* " Farewell and Adieu to you, Ladies of Spain," " Cawsand Bay," " The Coasts of High Barbary," etc., all of which have been repeatedly published.

A reference to the Notes will show that thirty-nine of the chanteys in this Collection have already seen the light in some form or other. The remaining twenty-one are, I believe, now published for the first time.

Fifty-seven of the chanteys in my Collection, and forty-six of those in this volume, were sung to me by Mr. John Short of Watchet, Somerset. Although seventy-six years of age he is apparently, so far as physical activity and mental alertness go, still in the prime of life. He has, too, the folk-singer's tenacious memory and, although I am sure he does not know it, very great musical ability of the uncultivated, unconscious order. He now holds the office of Town Crier in his native town, presumably on account of his voice, which is rich, resonant and powerful, and yet so flexible that he can execute trills, turns and graces with a delicacy and finish that would excite the envy of many a professed vocalist. Mr. Short has spent more than fifty years in sailing-ships and throughout the greater part of his career was a recognised chanteyman, i.e. the solo-singer who led the chanteys. It would be difficult, I imagine, to find a more experienced exponent of the art of chantey-singing, and I account myself peculiarly fortunate in having made his acquaintance in the course of my investigations and won his generous assistance. Of the other singers who have been good enough to sing to me, Mr. Perkins of St. Ives and the late Mr. Robbins of London deserve especial mention. The former gave me "Lowlands Low" (No. 29); while Mr. Robbins contributed twenty or more to my Collection including a remarkable variant of "Sally Brown" (No. 28).

The chantey may be defined as a song used by sailors during their work and devised, not only to keep them amused, but also, by assuring unanimity of action, to aid them in the efficient execution of their collective task. To understand the function of the chantey let us imagine a squad of men engaged in shifting a heavy weight. We shall then understand how greatly their task would be facilitated if by some means or other, e.g. a song, they were enabled to exert their united strength at precisely the same moment. A simple way of securing this end was explained to me by a practical seaman, who told me that on such occasions he would recite, slowly and impressively and to the following rhythm, this sentence,

I sell brooms, squee-gees and swabs.

instructing the men to make their effort on the word "swabs."

In this example we have the germ of the chantey; it may be said indeed that the most elaborate pulling-chantey is no more than a highly developed extension of this simple verbal formula.

Now all formal and public utterances, if constantly repeated, tend in course of time to take on some measure of artistic embellishment. The street-vendor, for instance, perpetually reiterating in a loud voice the same cry, will sooner or later instinctively call music to his aid and sing or chant his words. Many of the Street Cries, e.g. "London Lavender," are quite beautiful (see Folk-Song Society's Journal, IV, p. 97), and most of them have been handed down by tradition for many generations. Again, the short musical phrase with which sailors announce the reading of the lead-line is another instance in point. Mr. Henry Bailey, a Bridgwater sailor, sang me the following phrases :—

A quar-ter less five   Hand and a half six

Mr. Perkins of St. Ives gave me more elaborate versions, as follows :—

By the deep nine—I wish that girl was mine   Six no bot-tom—There she is passing a-long.

 Mr. Perkins explained that the second phrase of each of the above cries was sung *sotto voce* to the crew and was not intended to be overheard by the captain or pilot.

I have been told, too, that the bargees on the Severn use a pole to take soundings, and that when the depth of the water is greater than the length of the pole the fact is recorded in the following words :—

> No ground,
> No sound,
> No bottom to be found
> With a long, pitch-pine pole, daddy O.

These lines are not, it is true, chanted—except perhaps in a monotone—yet here again in the rhyming, alliteration and the rhythmical cadence of the syllables we have another example of the same tendency.

The chantey, however, differs in many respects from the examples just quoted. It is essentially a collective, not an individual, performance, and it must therefore be differentiated from the song which the solitary worker (the painter, cobbler or stone-breaker) will whistle or sing to while away the time—a song which has nothing whatever to do with the character or the efficient execution of his work.

There are two kinds of chanteys, the Capstan-chantey, and the Pulling-chantey.

The first of these, the capstan-chantey, is used to accompany work of a regular rhythmical character, *e.g.* marching round the capstan, working the pumps, etc. Soldiers' marching songs, rowing-songs and the waulking-songs of the Scottish weavers are labour-songs of a similar type. Occupations of this kind give rise to regular, rhythmical movements and these can advantageously be accompanied, and the movements emphasised, by any song in which the metrical accents follow one another at the required pace. A large number of chanteys belong to this class. In form, the capstan-chantey consists of a solo and chorus, the precentor, or chanteyman, singing the verse and the workers the refrain. Occasionally, solo and refrain are sung to alternate lines of the text, as in " Heave away my Johnny " (No. 26) ; but more often the chorus follows the completion of each stanza as in " Whip Jamboree " (No. 9), " Farewell and Adieu to you, Ladies of Spain," etc. No specialised form of song is needed for this purpose. Any ballad will serve so long as the tune can be sung at the required *tempo* and the words are calculated to hold the attention of the sailors.

It is otherwise with the pulling-chantey which must be sharply distinguished from the type just described. The capstan-chantey is sung, as we have seen, when the work is continuous and sustained ; but the pulling-chantey is used to accompany work that is irregular or spasmodic, as, for instance, when a succession of hard pulls is required to raise the yards, hoist the sails, etc.

Now if work of this kind is to be effectively executed, and with due economy of effort—(1) the pulls must be made in perfect accord ; (2) regular intervals for rest must be allowed between the pulls to enable the workers to take a fresh grip of the rope, to recover their breath and conserve their strength ; and (3) the song must interest the sailors and occupy their attention. A reference to " Reuben Ranzo " (No. 32) will show how the pulling-chantey satisfies these requirements. The soloist, *i.e.* the chanteyman, first of all sings, by way of introduction, the refrain, or a shortened form of it ; this is to announce the chantey he has chosen and to remind his hearers of the tune. This was not an invariable practice though it was very commonly observed. The soloist then chants the first line, " O poor old Reuben Ranzo," to which the sailors reply " *Ranzo*, boys, *Ranzo*," pulling as they sing the italicised syllables. These two lines are then repeated to the second phrase of the tune, so that the sailors get in two double-pulls in the course of the stanza. Pulling-chanteys are not all constructed in this way. Sometimes, as for instance in " Haul away, Joe," a single- is substituted for the double-pull and a regular and lengthened refrain is interpolated between the stanzas. But whatever form it may take, the pulling-chantey, with one exception, always consists of a periodic series of single or dual-pulls. The exception is in those special operations in which one pull only is needed, as, for instance, when a sail is " bunted." In this case, as I understand it, the work is prepared beforehand, after which the single strong pull that is required to complete the job is executed with the aid of the chantey. I have been told, too, that in raising a yard the first part of the work is not " chanteyed " because, being easy, it can be effected by one continuous effort.* It is only when the yard has very nearly reached its haven and a few very powerful pulls (technically known as " sweating up " or " punishment ") are all that are needed to finish the operation, that the aid of the chantey is invoked. Again, if the job is a

* Occasionally, even this part of the work was accompanied by a song of the capstan type, usually known as a " walk-away " chantey (See Note to No.).

peculiarly tough one, a single pull is substituted for a double one. Sometimes this second pull is omitted for no other reason than that the men are interested in the chantey—perhaps the chanteyman is in a specially happy and amusing vein—and they want to make the work last as long as possible.

To the sailor the chief attraction of the chantey was that it infected his work with the spirit of play—as a chanteyman once said to me, " It was only just a few words we had, but it made the thing come lighter." Although the words of the refrains were often mere jingles, a succession of more or less meaningless syllables, they served their purpose none the less on that account. It was in the tune that the interest lay, and the words were little more than pegs upon which to hang the notes. With the words of the soloist it was otherwise, for these were improvised and it was the excitement which this aroused that riveted the attention of the workers. It was for this reason, no doubt, that a clever chanteyman was accounted a valuable asset in a ship's crew—it used to be said in the Merchant Service* that a capable chanteyman was worth a couple of extra hands. He was a " privileged " person, at any rate on some ships, and was given light and easy jobs and released from duty whenever possible. In most chanteys, *e.g.* " Ranzo," it is one line only in each stanza that has to be improvised, so that the demands made upon the singer's powers of invention are not overwhelming. Every chanteyman, too, has a number of stock lines, or " tags," stored up in his memory, such as—" Up aloft this yard must go," " I think I heard the old man (*i.e.* the captain) say "—upon which he can always draw when inspiration fails him. The paucity of singable words vitiates to some extent the practical value of a Collection such as this ; on the other hand it should not be difficult for the amateur to emulate the chanteyman and invent words of his own.

It should, perhaps, be added that the words in the text are those that were actually sung to me. I have not "edited" them in any way beyond excising a few lines and softening two or three expressions.

Traditionally, the chantey is sung very slowly and deliberately and the tune embellished—especially by the chanteyman himself—with numberless trills and graces, with every now and again a curious catch in the voice (a kind of hiccough), and numerous falsetto notes. These embellishments are highly characteristic, but they are very difficult, and the amateur would be well advised not to attempt to imitate them. He must remember, however, to sing the chanteys slowly and impressively and, the majority of them at any rate, without accompaniment. Accompaniments, it is true, are given in the text, but this is only that the melodies may, if required, be played as instrumental airs.

The origin of the chantey-tune is a question beset with difficulty. A great many of the airs—I should be inclined to say a majority of them—must

---

* The singing of chanteys was not permitted in the Navy.

originally have been drawn from the stock of peasant-tunes with which the memory of every country-bred sailor would naturally be stored. In most cases these have, in the process of adaptation, undergone many changes, although there are instances where the folk-ballad has been "lifted" bodily into the service of the chantey without any alteration whatever, as for example "Blow away the Morning Dew" (Whall, p. 35) and "Sweet Nightingale" (*Songs of the West*, No. 15). The latter was given me as a capstan-chantey by Mr. Short who told me that he had himself converted it into a chantey, and that it had always become a favourite with the crews he had sailed with.

Very often too—for the sailors' taste is comprehensive rather than particular—popular street-songs were added to the sailors' repertory of chanteys, *e.g.* "Champagne Charlie," "Doo-dah-day," etc.

Another source, too, from which the chantey seems to have been replenished is the hymn-book; at any rate there are many chanteys that have hymn-tune characteristics, *e.g.* "Leave her Johnny" (No. 3), etc. The resemblance may be adventitious, *i.e.* the short, concise phrases peculiar to the chantey may have led naturally to the construction of tunes of this character; or, on the other hand, as the sailor is a great singer of hymn-tunes of the more emotional type, it may be that he has consciously or unconsciously introduced some of the phrases of his favourite tunes into the chantey.

Lastly, there is the vexed question of negro influence. Mr. Arnold, the musical editor of Mr. Bullen's Collection, holds that "the majority of the chanteys are negroid in origin." I cannot subscribe to this opinion, although I admit that the negro has undoubtedly left his impress upon a certain number of chantey-tunes. The technical peculiarities of negroid music are not easy to define with precision. Mr. A. H. Fox Strangways has, however, drawn my attention to the prevalence in negro music of the "melodic-third," *i.e.* of a shape of melody which implies a preference for harmonising in thirds, instead of the fourth, which is, of course, the basic interval of European folk-song (*see* the opening phrase of 'Mudder Dinah' in Mr. Bullen's Collection). Then there is that characteristic form of syncopated rhythm, popularly known as "rag-time," which, however, although undoubtedly negro in origin, is found very rarely, if at all, in the chantey. And, finally, there is the fondness of the negro for musical "patter," *i.e.* for passages consisting of a number of short, quick notes, each with its separate syllable.

That the chantey should have been affected by the negro is not surprising when we remember that sailing-ships, engaged in the Anglo-American trade, commonly carried "chequered" crews, *i.e.* one watch of coloured men and one of white. It is necessary, however, to distinguish between music of negroid origin and European music that has been modified by the negro. "Sing, Sally O" (No. 31) is an instance in point. Mr. Bullen prints a variant of this, "Mudder Dinah" (No. 1), and dubs it, without hesitation, a "negro chanty." This, no doubt, is true of the words, but surely not of the tune, which is a close variant of "Haul away, Joe" (No. 27), an air which is singularly devoid of negro characteristics, and one, moreover, which, it has been said, is "one of our oldest chantey-tunes" (*see* Folk-Song Society's *Journal*, V, p. 32). Again, "Santy Anna," "Whip Jamboree," "He-Back, She-Back" and "Clear the Track" (Nos. 1, 9, 4 and 6) are all variations of the Irish folk-tune "Shule Agra," yet the last three of these all display characteristics for which the American negro must obviously be held responsible.

However, I do not wish to be dogmatic. Sufficient material has not yet been amassed upon which to found a sound theory of the origin of the chantey-tune; and it may be that when further evidence is available the somewhat speculative opinions above expressed will need material modification.

C. J. S.

Dragonfield,
    Uxbridge.

CAPSTAN CHANTEYS

I. SANTY ANNA.

Santy Anna run away; Horoo, Santy Anna;

Santa Anna run away All on the plains of Mexico

SANTY ANNA.

2.   General Taylor gained the day,

3.   Mexico you all do know,

4.   The Americans 'll make Ureta* fly,

* i.e. Huerta.

II. LEAVE HER JOHNNY.

FIRST VERSION.

O the times are hard and the wa-ges low; Leave her John-ny leave her; O the times are hard and the wa-ges low, It's time for us to leave her.

LEAVE HER JOHNNY.

2. The bread is hard and the beef is salt,

3. O, a leaking ship and a harping crew,

4. Our mate he is a bully man,
   He gives us all the best he can.

5. I've got no money, I've got no clothes,

6. O, my old mother she wrote to me:

7. I will send you money, I will send you clothes.

III. LEAVE HER JOHNNY.

SECOND VERSION.

The times are hard and the wa - ges low, Leave her John - ny leave her, O the

times are hard and the wa - ges low, It's time for us to leave her.

LEAVE HER JOHNNY.

2. The bread is hard and the beef is salt,

3. O, a leaking ship and a harping crew,

4. Our mate he is a bully man,
   He gives us all the best he can.

5. I've got no money, I've got no clothes,

6. O, my old mother she wrote to me:

7. I will send you money, I will send you clothes.

IV. HE - BACK, SHE - BACK.

He - back, she - back, dad - dy shot a bear, Shot him in the back and he

ne - ver turned a hair, I'm just from the rail - road, too - rer - loo, O the

CHORUS.

old moke pick - ing on the ban - jo.   Hoo - roo! What's the mat - ter now? I'm

just from the rail - road, too - rer - loo, I'm just from the rail - road,

too - rer - loo, O the old moke pick - ing on the ban - jo.

V. THE HOG-EYED MAN.

Solo.

O who's been here since I've been gone? Some big black nig-ger with his

Chorus.

sea - boots on, And a hog - eye,   Stead-y up a jig   and a hog - eye,

Stead-y up a jig,   And all   she wants   is   her   hog - eyed   man.

THE HOG-EYED MAN.

2.   The hog-eyed man is the man for me,
He brought me down from Tennessee.

VI. CLEAR THE TRACK.

I wish I was in Lon-don town; Ha-hee, ha-oo, are you most done; I wish I was in Lon-don town; So clear away the track and let the bull-gine run. With my hi-rig-a-jig and a low-back car, Ha-hee, ha-oo, are you most done, To my pret-ty lit-tle yal-ler girl fare thee well, So clear away the track and let the bull-gine run.

2. 'Twas there I saw the girls around.

VII. DRUNKEN SAILOR.

2.   Put him in the long-boat till he gets sober.

3.   Keep him there and make him bail her.

VIII. DO LET ME GO.

It's of a mer-chant's daugh - ter be-longed to Cal - li - o;...... Hoo-

- raw,...... my yal - ler girls, do...... let me go........

Do ..... let me go, ... girls, Do...... let me go,........ Hoo-

- raw,...... my yal - ler girls, do...... let me go........

IX. WHIP JAMBOREE.

Solo.

Now Cape Clear it is in ... sight, We'll be off Ho-ly-head by to-

-mor-row night, And we'll shape our course for the Rock Light; O ...

Jen-ny get your oat-cake done.

Chorus.

Whip jam-bo-ree, whip

jam-bo-ree, O you long-tailed black man poke it up be-hind me, Whip

jam - bo - ree, Whip jam - bo - ree, O .. Jen-ny get your oat - cake done.

colla voce.

WHIP JAMBOREE.

2. Now my lads, we're round the Rock,
   All hammocks lashed and chests all locked,
   We'll haul her into the Waterloo Dock,
   O, Jenny, get your oat-cake done.

3. Now, my lads, we're all in dock
   We'll be off to Dan Lowrie's on the spot ;
   And now we'll have a good roundabout,
   O, Jenny, get your oat-cake done.

X. ROLL AND GO.

ROLL AND GO.

2.   O, Sally Brown's the girl for me,
     O, Sally Brown, she slighted me.

3.   As I walked out one morning fair,
     It's then I met her, I do declare.

XI. SHANADAR.

FIRST VERSION.

O Shan - a - dar I love your daugh - ter, Hoo - ray you rol - ling

ri - ver. Shan - a - dar I love your daugh - ter Ha

Ha.... I'm bound a - way to the wild Mis - sou - ri.

SHANADAR.

2. O seven years I courted Sally.

3. And seven more I couldn't gain her.

4. She said I was a tarry sailor.

5. Farewell my dear I'm bound to leave you;
   I'm bound away but will ne'er deceive you.

13

XII. ROLLER, BOWLER.

Hoo - ray you rol - ler, bow - ler; To my hi - rig - a - jig and a ha ha. Good morn - ing la - dies all.

(1.) O the first time that I
(2.) As I walked out one

saw her, Hoo - ray...... you rol - ler, bow - ler; O the
morn - ing, Hoo - ray...... you rol - ler, bow - ler; As

first time that I saw her 'Twas down in Play - house Square, To my
I walked out one morn - ing, Down by the ri - ver side,

hi - rig - a - jig and a ha ha. Good morn - ing la - dies all.

Chorus.

Hoo - ray.... you rol - ler, bow - ler; To my hi - rig - a - jig and a

ha ha Good morn ing la - dies all. (3.) O la - dies short and la - dies tall, Hoo -

Solo.

- ray you rol - ler, bow-ler; O la - dies short and la-dies tall I love them

15

all, To my hi-rig-a-jig and a ha ha. Good morn-ing la-dies all.

XIII. LET THE BULLGINE RUN.

We'll run from night till.. morn - ing. O run, let the bull-gine

run. Way - yah, oo - oo oo-oo-oo, O .. run, let the bull-gine run.

LET THE BULLGINE RUN.

2. We'll run from Dover to Calais.

3. We sailed away from Mobile Bay.

4. We gave three cheers and away we went.

5. Now up aloft this yard must go.

6. We're homeward bound for Liverpool Docks.

XIV. HUCKLEBERRY HUNTING.

SOLO.

The boys and the girls went a - huc - kle - ber - ry

CHORUS.

hunt - ing; To my way - ay ay - ay ay - ay

SOLO.

yah; All the boys.. and the girls went a - huc - kle - ber - ry

CHORUS.

hunt - ing: To my Hi - lo, my Ran - zo - ray.

XV. ONE MORE DAY.

One more day, my John-ny, one more day; O rock and roll me o - ver For one more day.

(1.) There is one thing more that grieves me For one more day There is
(2.) I'm bound a - way to leave you For one more day Don't

my poor wife and ba - by For one more day.
let my part - ing grieve you For one more day.

18

XVI. O JOHNNY COME TO HILO.

O a poor old.. man came a - ri - ding by, Says I: old man your

horse will die. O John-ny come to Hi - lo, O poor old man.

O wake her, O shake her, O shake that girl with the

blue dress on, O John-ny come to Hi - lo; Poor old man.

XVII. GOOD MORNING, LADIES ALL.

Solo. (Introduction)

Aye yo............. o, aye yo............ o. I thought I heard our cap-tain say: Aye.... yo............ o, aye yo............. o. O go on board your pi-lot boat And roll her down the bay. Ha, ha, my yal-ler girls, Good morning, la-dies all.

    2.   Our Captain on the quarter-deck (*bis*)
        Was looking very sad.

XVIII. LOWLANDS AWAY.

Low-lands, low-lands a-way, my John; I'm bound a-way, I heard him say, My dol-lar and a half a day. A dol-lar and a half won't pay my way; Low-lands, low-lands a-way, my John; A dol-lar and a half is a oozer's pay, A dollar and a half a day.

LOWLANDS AWAY.

2. A dollar and a half won't pay my way ;
   A dollar and a half is a white-man's pay.

3. We're bound away to Mobile Bay ; (*bis*)

4. What shall we poor matelors do ? (*bis*)

XIX. THE BULLY BOAT.

Ah the bul - ly boat is com - ing, Don't you hear the pad - dles

rol - ling? Ran - do, ran - do, hoo - ray, hoo -

- ray; The bul - ly boat is com - ing, Don't you hear the pad - dles

rol - ling? Ran - do, ran - do, ray.

2. Ah! the bully boat is coming,
Down the Mississippi floating.

3. As I walked out one May morning
To hear the steam-boat rolling.

XX. STORMALONG JOHN.

I wish I was old Stor-my's son; To my way........ ay............

Storm - a - long John. I wish I was old Stor - my's son, Ha,

ha, come a - long, get a - long, Stor - my a - long John.

STORMALONG JOHN.

2. I'd give those sailors lots of rum.

3. O was you ever in Quebec?

4. A-stowing timber on the deck.

5. I wish I was in Baltimore.

6. On the grand old American shore.

23

XXI. RIO GRAND.

I think I heard the old man say: O........ you Ri - o, ... I

think I heard the old.. man say: We're bound for Ri - o Grand......

And a - way........ for Ri - o, ... O.......... you Ri - o, ... So

fare you well, my bon - ny young girl, We're bound for Ri - o Grand......

2. O Rio Grand is my native land.

3. It's there that I would take my stand.

4. She's a buxom young maid with a rolling black eye.

5. She came from her dwelling a long way from here.

6. I wish I was in Rio to-day.

7. Buckle* sailors you'll see there, With long sea-boats and close cropped hair.

* i.e. swell and rowdy.

XXII. LUCY LONG.

Was you e - - ver on.... the Brum - a - low, Where the

Yan - kee boys are all the go? To my way - - ay - -

- ay - - - - ha, ha; ...... My John - ny, boys, ha ha..........

Why .... don't you try for to wring Miss Lu - cy Long?

2. O! as I walked out one morning fair,
To view the views and take the air.

3. 'Twas there I met Miss Lucy fair,
'Twas there we met I do declare.

XXIII. THE BLACK BALL LINE.

In Tap-scott's line we're bound to shine; A - way...... Hoo - ray, Yah; In

Tap - scott's line we're bound for to shine, Hoo - ray for the Black Ball Line.

THE BLACK BALL LINE.

2.   In the Black Ball Line I served my time.

3.   We sailed away from Liverpool Bay.

4.   We sailed away for Mobile Bay.

5.   It was there we discharged our cargo, boys.

6.   We loaded cotton for the homeward bound.

7.   And when we arrived at Liverpool Dock.

8.   We ran our lines on to the pier.

9.   We made her fast all snug and taut.

10.   The skipper said : That will do, my boys.

XXIV. FIRE ! FIRE !

There is fire in the gal-ley, There is fire down be-low,

Fetch a buck-et of wa-ter, girls, There's fire down be-low. Fire ! Fire !

Fire down be-low. It's fetch a buck-et of wa-ter, girls, There's fire down be-low.

FIRE ! FIRE !

2.   There is fire in the fore-top,
There's fire in the main ;
Fetch a bucket of water, girls,
And put it out again.

3.   As I walked out one morning fair
All in the month of June.
I overheard an Irish girl
A-singing this old tune.

XXV. A - ROVING.

In Plymouth town there lived a maid; Bless you, young wo - men; In
Ply - mouth town there lived a maid; O mind what I do say; In
Ply - mouth town there lived a maid, And she was mis - tress of her trade; I'll
go no more a - ro - ving with you, fair maid.

A - ROVING.

2. I took this fair maid for a walk,
   And we had such a loving talk.

3. I took her hand within my own,
   And said : I'm bound to my old home.

The lines "Bless you, young women" and "O mind what I do say" are sometimes sung in chorus.

XXVI. HEAVE AWAY, MY JOHNNY.

It's of a farm-er's daugh-ter, so beau-ti-ful I'm told; Heave a-way .... my John-ny, heave a-way .... Her fa-ther died and left ...... her five hun-dred pound in gold; Heave a-way .... my bon-ny boys, We're all bound a-way ....

2. Her uncle and the squire rode out one summer's day. (*bis*)
3. Young William is in favour, her uncle he did say. (*bis*)

PULLING CHANTEYS

XXVII. HAUL AWAY, JOE.

Haul a - way, haul a - way, haul a - way, my Ro - sie,

Way, haul a - way, haul a - way, Joe. O you talk a - bout your A - ver* girls, And

round the cor - ner Sal - ly; Way, haul a - way, haul a - way, Joe.

* i.e. Havre.

2. But they cannot come to tea
With the girls in Booble Alley.

3. O! once I loved a nigger girl,
And I loved her for her money.

4. O! once I had a nice young girl,
And she was all a posy.

5. And now I've got an English girl,
I treat her like a lady.

6. We sailed away for the East Indies,
With spirits light and gay.

7. We discharge our cargo there, my boys.
And we took it light and easy.

8. We loaded for our homeward bound,
With the winds so free and easy.

9. We squared our yards and away we ran,
With the music playing freely.

10. Now, up aloft this yard must go,
We'll pull her free and easy.

11. Another pull and then belay,
We'll make it all so easy.

N.B.—*In this and the following chanteys arrow-heads are placed immediately over the notes upon which the pulls are made.*

XXVIII. SALLY BROWN.

I shipped on board of a Li-ver-pool li-ner; Way, ho, a-

-rol-ling go; And I shipped on board of a Li-ver-pool li-ner,

For I spent my mo-ney 'long with Sal-ly Brown.

SALLY BROWN.

2. O Sally Brown was a Creole lady.

3. O Sally Brown was a bright mulatto.

4. O seven years I courted Sally.

5. And now we're married and we're living nice and comfor'ble.

33

D

XXIX. LOWLANDS LOW.

Low - lands, Low - lands, Low - lands, low - lands, low.

Our Cap - tain is a bul - ly man; Low - lands, low - lands, low - lands low; He .. gave us bread as hard as brass; Low - lands, low - lands, low - lands low.

XXX. SHALLOW BROWN.

FIRST VERSION.

SHALLOW BROWN.

2. And who do you think was master of her?

3. A Yankee mate and a lime-juice skipper.

4. And what do you think they had for dinner?

5. A parrot's tail and a monkey's liver.

XXXI. SING, SALLY O.

SING, SALLY O.

2.   O have you heard the news to-day?
For we are homeward bound.

36

XXXII. POOR OLD REUBEN RANZO.

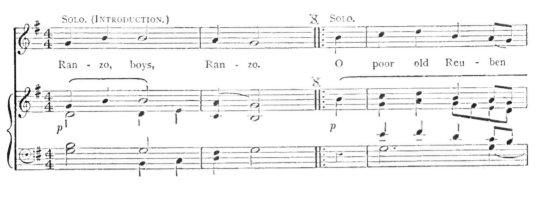

POOR OLD REUBEN RANZO.

2. O! Ranzo was no sailor.

3. He shipped on board a whaler.

4. He shipped with Captain Taylor.

5. The man that shot the sailor.

6. He could not do his duty.

7. He couldn't boil the coffee.

8. The Captain being a good man.

9. He taught him navigation.

10. We took him to the gratings.

11. And gave him nine and thirty.

12 O! that was the end of Ranzo.

XXXIII. GENERAL TAYLOR.

SOLO.
CHORUS.
(1.) Gen - e - ral Tay - lor gained the day; Walk him a - long, John - ny,
(2.) Dan O' Con - nell died long a - go; Walk him a - long, John - ny,
p
f
SOLO.
CHORUS.
car - ry him a - long. Gen - e - ral Tay - lor gained the day;
car - ry him a - long. Dan O' Con - nell died long a - go;
Car - ry him to the
p
f
CHORUS.
bu - ry - ing ground. Oo.. oo oo.... oo you stor - - my,
f
Walk him a - long, John - ny, car - ry him a - long; oo.... oo.. oo you....

stor — — my, Car - ry him to.... the bu - ry - ing ground.

XXXIV. OLD STORMEY.

Solo.
I wish I was old Stor-mey's son; To my way, yah, storm-a - long, I'd

Chorus.

Solo.

Chorus.

give those sai - lors lots of rum; Aye, aye, aye, Mis-ter Storm-a - long.

OLD STORMEY.

2. I'd build a ship both neat and strong
   To sail the world around all round.

3. Old Stormey's dead, I saw him die.

4. We dug his grave with a silver spade.

5. We lowered him down with a golden chain.

6. And now we'll sing his funeral song.

XXXV. BULLY IN THE ALLEY.

SOLO. CHORUS.

So help my bob I'm bul-ly in the al - ley; Way...... ay ....

SOLO. CHORUS.

bul - ly in the al - ley, So help my bob I'm bul-ly in the al - ley; Way .... ay ......

SOLO. CHORUS.

bul - ly in the al - ley. Bul-ly down in our al - ley; So help my bob I'm

bul - ly in the al - ley, Way...... ay........ bul - ly in the al · ley;

BULLY IN THE ALLEY.

2.   Have you seen our Sally ?

3.   She's the girl in the alley.

XXXVI. LIZA LEE.

XXXVII. HAUL ON THE BOW-LINE.

Haul on the bow-line, O Kit-ty you are my dar - ling, Haul on the bow-line, the bow - line, haul. Be - cause she had a fore - top, fore and main to bow - line; Haul on the bow-line, the bow - line haul. Be - cause she had a main - top main and mi-zen to bow - line; Haul the bow - line, the bow - line haul.

Haul on the bow-line, O Kit-ty you are my dar - ling, Haul on the bow-line, the bow-line haul.

XXXVIII. PADDY DOYLE.

CHORUS.

To my way - ay.... ay - ay.... ay - - -

- yah, We'll pay Pad - dy Doyle for his boots..... ....

PADDY DOYLE.

2. We'll order in brandy and gin.

3. We'll all throw dirt at the cook.

4. The dirty old man on the poop.

XXXIX.   KNOCK A MAN DOWN.

Knock a man down, kick a man down; way ay knock a man down,
knock a man down right down to the ground, O give me some time to
knock a man down. The watch-man's dog stood ten foot high;
Way ay knock a man down, The watch-man's dog stood

ten foot high; O give me some time to knock a man down.

KNOCK A MAN DOWN.

2. A lively ship and a lively crew.

3. O we are the boys to put her through

4. I wish I was in London Town.

5. It's there we'd make the girls fly round.

XL. JOHNNY BOWKER.

SOLO.

Do my John-ny Bow - ker, Come rock and roll me

CHORUS.

o - ver; Do my John-ny Bow - ker, do.

XLI. TIDDY I O.

O now you for-bid us to bid you a-dieu; Tid-dy I - o, I - o;..... O

now you for-bid us to bid you a-dieu; Tid-dy I - o, I - o, I - o.

TIDDY I O.

2. We're homeward bound to Bristol Town.

3. We're homeward bound with sugar and rum

4. And when we arrive in Bristol docks.

5. O then the people will come down in flocks.

XLII. ROUND THE CORNER, SALLY.

ROUND THE CORNER, SALLY.

2. O! I wish I was at Madame Gashees. (*bis*)

3. O! it's there, my boys, we'd take our ease.

XLIII. SO HANDY.

SO HANDY.

2. Be handy at your washing, girls.
3. My love she likes her brandy.
4. My love she is a dandy.
5. I thought I heard our Captain say :
6. At daylight we are bound away.
7. Bound away for Botany Bay.

XLIV. A LONG TIME AGO.

A LONG TIME AGO.

2. O! early on a summer's morn.

3. I made up my mind to go to sea.

XLV. CHEERLY MAN.

XLVI. THE SAILOR LIKES HIS BOTTLE O.

Solo (Introduction.)

So ear - ly in the morn - ing The sai - lor likes his bot - tle O.

Solo.

A bot - tle of rum and a bot - tle of gin, And a bot - tle of old Ja -

Chorus.

- mai - ca Ho! So ear - ly in the morn - ing The sai - lor likes his bot - tle O.

Dal segno.

p

f

XLVII. THE DEAD HORSE.

SOLO. A poor old man came a-rid-ing by, And they say so, and I
CHORUS.

hope so, A poor old man came a-rid-ing.. by, O poor old man.

THE DEAD HORSE.

2. Says I : Old man your horse will die.

3. And if he dies I'll tan his skin.

4. And if he don't I'll ride him again.

5. After very hard work and sore abuse.
   They salted me down for sailors' use.

6. And if you think my words not true,
   Just look in the cask and you'll find my shoe.

7. But our old horse is dead and gone,
   And we *know* so, and we *say* so,
     etc., etc.

XLVIII. WHISKY FOR MY JOHNNY.

WHISKY FOR MY JOHNNY.

2. I'll drink whisky while I can.

3. Whisky in an old tin can.

4. Whisky up and whisky down.

5. Pass the whisky all around.

6. Whisky polished my old nose.

7. Whisky made me go to sea.

8. My wife drinks whisky, I drink gin.

9. Whisky killed my mam and dad.

10. Whisky killed our whole ship's crew.

11. Whisky made me pawn my shirt.

XLIX. BONNY WAS A WARRIOR.

BONNY WAS A WARRIOR.

2. Bonny went to Moscow.

3. Moscow was on fire.

4. It took the Duke of Wellington

5. O to defeat old Bonny.

6. Hurrah, hurrah, for Bonny.

7. A bully, fighting terrier.

L. BLOW, BOYS, COME BLOW TOGETHER.

Blow,   boys,   come blow to - ge-ther; Blow,   boys,   blow,

Blow,   boys, come blow   to - ge - ther; Blow, my bul - ly boys, blow.

BLOW, BOYS, COME BLOW TOGETHER.

    2.   A Yankee ship came down the river.

    3.   And who do you think was Master of her?

    4.   Why Bully Brag of New York City.

    5.   And what do you think we had for supper?

    6.   Belaying-pin soup and a roll in the gutter.

LI.   HANGING JOHNNY.

And they calls me hang-ing John-ny;..... Hoo-ray,......... hoo-

- ray.   And they calls me Hang-ing John-ny,....   So hang, boys, hang.

HANGING JOHNNY.

2.   They hanged my poor old father.

3.   They hanged my poor old mother.

4.   They say I hanged for money.

5.   But I never hanged nobódy.

LII. A HUNDRED YEARS ON THE EASTERN SHORE.

A hun-dred years on the east-ern shore; O yes O, And a

hun-dred years on the east-ern shore; A hun-dred years a - go.

A HUNDRED YEARS ON THE EASTERN SHORE.

2. A hundred years have passed and gone.

3. And a hundred years will come once more.

LIII. SHANADAR.

SECOND VERSION.

Shan - a - dar is a rol - ling ri - ver,   E -

- o........ I - o......... E - o........ I - o........

LIV. IN FRISCO BAY.

In Fris - co bay there lay three ships To my way - ay - ay - o, In

Fris - co bay there lay three ships A long time a - go.........

IN FRISCO BAY.

2. And one of those ships was Noah's old Ark,
   And covered all over with hickory bark.

3. They filled up the seams with oakum pitch.

4. And Noah of old commanded this Ark.

5. They took two animals of every kind.

6. The bull and the cow they started a row.

7. Then said old Noah with a flick of his whip:
   Come stop this row or I'll scuttle the ship.

8. But the bull put his horn through the side of the Ark;
   And the little black dog he started to bark.

9. So Noah took the dog, put his nose in the hole;
   And ever since then the dog's nose has been cold.

LV. SHALLOW BROWN.

O I'm going to leave her Shal - low O Shal - low Brown.

O I'm going to leave her Shal - low O Shal - low Brown.

SHALLOW BROWN.

2. Going away to-morrow,
   Bound away to-morrow.

3. Get my traps in order.

4. Ship on board a whaler.

5. Bound away to St. George's.

6. Love you well, Julianda.

7. Massa going to sell me.

8. Sell me to a Yankee.

9. Sell me for the dollar,
   Great big Spanish dollar.

LVI. WON'T YOU GO MY WAY.

I met her in the morn-ing; Won't you go my way? I
met her in the morn-ing; Won't you go my way?

WON'T YOU GO MY WAY.

2. In the morning bright and early.

3. O Julia, Anna, Maria.

4. I asked that girl to marry.

5. She said she'd rather tarry.

6. Oh marry, never tarry.

LVII.   WO, STORMALONG.

WO, STORMALONG.

2.   And Liverpool that Yankee School.

3.   And when you go to Playhouse Square,

4.   My bonny girl she do live there.

5.   We're bound away this very day.

6.   We're bound away at the break of day.

LVIII. O BILLY RILEY.

O Bil-ly Ri - ley, lit-tle Bil-ly Ri - ley, O Bil-ly Ri - ley O;

O Bil-ly Ri - ley, wake him up so cheer'-ly, O Bil-ly Ri - ley O.

O BILLY RILEY.

2.   O Mister Riley, O Missus Riley.

3.   O Miss Riley, O Billy Riley.

4.   O Miss Riley, screw him up so cheer'ly.

LIX. TOM IS GONE TO HILO.

My Tom is gone, what shall I do? Oo - way,   you I - o - o - o,   My

Tom is gone, what shall I   do? My Tom is gone to Hi - lo.

LX. TOMMY'S GONE AWAY.

Tom - my's gone, what shall   I   do?   Tom - my's gone   a - way,

Tom - my's gone, what shall   I   do?   Tom - my's gone   a - way.

NOTES

No. 1. SANTY ANNA.

Sung by Mr. John Short, at Watchet.

NTONIO LOPEZ DE SANTA ANNA (1795-1876) was a Mexican general, politician and conspirator. He led an adventurous life and was several times President of Mexico. He defeated the Spanish at Zampico and conducted a spirited defence of Vera Cruz against the French. On the outbreak of the war with the United States (1846) he took command of the Mexican troops, but was badly defeated by Generals Taylor and Scott and sent into exile. Recalled in 1853, he was again made President, this time for life, but was driven from power two years later. On the re-establishment of the Republic he attempted to overturn it but was captured and sentenced to death (1867), being pardoned on condition that he proceeded to the United States. Here he remained until the amnesty of 1872 permitted his return to Mexico, where he lived until his death in 1876.

For other versions of this chantey see F.S.S. *Journal*, iii, p. 236 and v, p. 33 ; Whall's *Sea Songs and Shanties*, p. 89 ; Tozer's *Sailors' Songs*, p. 40 ; Miss Smith's *Music of the Waters* : and Bullen's *Songs of Labour*, No. 35. I have taken down three versions, all modal, either dorian or, as in the present case, lacking the sixth note of the scale.

Nos. 2 & 3.   LEAVE HER JOHNNY, LEAVE HER.

First version sung by Mr. John Short, at Watchet.

Second version sung by Mr. Richard Perkins, at St. Ives.

This chantey was usually sung when getting into port, the chantey-man seizing this opportunity to express the crew's dissatisfaction with the ship they were about to leave, which, Mr. Bullen says, was very often fully justified. Mr. Short's variant, which is the usual form of the air, is very similar to the versions printed by Bullen (No. 9) and Tozer (No. 5). The first phrase of Mr. Perkins's variant, which is in the dorian mode, recalls the opening phrase of " I'm Seventeen come Sunday " (*Folk Songs from Somerset*, No. 29).

No. 4. HE-BACK, SHE-BACK.
Sung by Mr. John Short, at Watchet.

The tune, which is in the dorian mode, is, as Miss Gilchrist has pointed out to me, a variant of Shule Agra. " Hoo-roo " may be a reminiscence of " Shule Agra," and the reference to " the railroad " a memory of " Poor Paddy works on the railway." Both words and tune show negro influence. The chantey is not included in any other collection.

No. 5. THE HOG-EYED MAN.
Sung by Mr. John Short, at Watchet.

For other versions see Whall (p. 118) ; Tozer (No. 44) ; Bullen (No. 20) ; and F.S.S. *Journal* (ii, p. 248, and iii, p. 43). The tune of this chantey shows negro influence, especially in the curious and characteristic rhythm of the chorus.

No. 6. CLEAR THE TRACK.
Sung by Mr. George Conway, at London.

The tune, the final cadence of which is very similar to that of Santy Anna, is clearly related to that of Shule Agra (*Songs of the Four Nations*, p. 210) and of " Geordie " (*Folk Songs from Somerset*, No. 2). A Northumberland variant, collected by Mr. R. R. Terry, is printed in *A Book of British Song* (No. 16). See also *The Yachting Monthly* (Oct., 1906) ; Miss Smith's *Music of the Waters*, p 46 ; and " Eliza Lee " in Tozer's *Sailors' Songs or Chanties* (No. 12).

No. 7   THE DRUNKEN SAILOR.
Sung by Mr. James Tucker, at Bristol.

The tune in the text—obviously a bagpipe air—is in a six-note mode.

The following variant, in the æolian mode, was sung to me by Mr. Conway, of London :

If the signature of this air be changed to one sharp, the tune becomes a mixolydian one and in this form (except for one unimportant note) it was sung to me in London by Mr. George Humphreys.

Tozer (No. 24) prints a major version of the air ; Whall (p. 107) a dorian, and Bullen (No. 17) a mixolydian variant identical with Mr. Humphreys's version, quoted above, which may, I think, be regarded as the normal form of the tune.

Mr. Fleetwood Stileman tells me that this chantey (chorus only) was very commonly sung as the sailors tramped along the deck in raising a yard, or rather during the first and easier stage of that operation (see also Masefield's *Sailor's Garland*, p. 301).

No. 8. DO LET ME GO.
Sung by Mr. John Short, at Watchet.

I have not heard this chantey from any one but Mr. Short, nor, so far as I know, is it printed elsewhere. The tune is in the mixolydian mode. Mr. Short always sang "*doodle* let me go."

No. 9. WHIP JAMBOREE.
Sung by Mr. John Short, at Watchet.

I know of no other version of this chantey except one, in the major mode, given me by Mr. George Conway. The tune, which is in the æolian mode, is a variant of Santy Anna (No. 1). In its construction, and to some extent in the character of its words, the chantey is akin to Spanish Ladies (*Folk Songs from Somerset*, No. 124). The words of the chorus show negro influence. The Rock Light is in Cheshire, at the mouth of the Mersey. "Old Dan Lowrie's," Mr. Short said, was a popular playhouse in Paradise Street, Liverpool, near the Waterloo Dock, much frequented by sailors.

No. 10. ROLL AND GO.
Sung by Mr. John Short, at Watchet.

I know nothing about this chantey, having noted it from no one else than Mr. Short. The tune shows mixolydian influence.

No. 11. SHANADAR.
Sung by Mr. John Short, at Watchet.

For other versions see F.S.S. *Journal* (ii. 247 and v. 44); *Music of the Waters* (p. 51); Whall (p. 1); Tozer (No. 4); Bullen (No. 10); and Bradford and Fagge's *Old Sea Chanties*. The chantey is a famous one and seems to be universally known to sailors. The tune is always irregular in its rhythm. Shenandoah was, I believe, a celebrated Indian Chief, after whom a Pennsylvanian town and one of the branches of the Potomac river are named.

No. 12. ROLLER BOWLER.
Sung by Mr. John Short, at Watchet.

I have no variants of this chantey and I know of no other printed version of it.

No. 13. LET THE BULLGINE RUN.

Sung by Mr. John Short, at Watchet.

Versions of this chantey are published by Bullen (No. 36) and Tozer (No. 24). "Bullgine" is, I believe, nigger slang for "engine."

No. 14. HUCKLEBERRY HUNTING.

Sung by Mr. John Short, at Watchet.

Whall (p. 131) prints a version of this chantey with very much the same words, and Bullen (No. 19) and Tozer (No. 26) versions of the tune set to other words.

No. 15. ONE MORE DAY.

Sung by Mr. John Short, at Watchet.

Mr. Short told me he always used this as a capstan or windlass-chantey, but Bullen (No. 25) and Whall (p. 77) give it as a pulling-chantey and Tozer (No. 36) as one for pumping. Mr. Whall calls it a "homeward-bound shanty."

No. 16. O JOHNNY COME TO HILO.

Sung by Mr. John Short, at Watchet.

Versions of this chantey are given by Bullen (No. 10) and Tozer (No. 42). Presumably, Hilo is the seaport of that name on the east coast of Hawaii Island.

No. 17. GOOD MORNING LADIES ALL.

Sung by Mr. John Short, at Watchet.

I know of no variant of this chantey. The tune has some affinity with "Heave away my Johnny" (No. 26).

No. 18. LOWLANDS AWAY.

Sung by Mr. Henry Bailey, at Bridgwater.

This is a well known chantey, but usually a troublesome one to transcribe on account of its irregular rhythm ; Mr. Bailey's version, however, presented no difficulty of this kind. Other variants are printed in F.S.S. *Journal* (iii, 233) ; Whall (p. 81) ; Tozer (No. 10) ; Bullen (No. 13) ; and *Music of the Waters* (p. 15).

The words of the fourth verse were given me by Mr. Short. "Matelors" means "sailors," as Mr. Short well knew ; and an "oozer," he said, was a cotton stevedore.

No. 19. THE BULLY BOAT.
Sung by Mr. John Short, at Watchet.

I collected a variant of this chantey at Newcastle which is printed in the F.S.S. *Journal* (v, 40) together with a Lancashire variant collected by Miss Gilchrist. Miss Gilchrist suggests that the tune is the air upon which "Off to Philadelphia" was founded.

Mr. Short always sang "rodeling" for "rolling."

No. 20. STORMALONG, JOHN.
Sung by Mr. John Short, at Watchet.

This is apparently an entirely different chantey from "Old Stormey" (No. 34) although the words of the first two verses are the same. I know of no variants except one given by Miss Smith (p. 16).

No. 21. RIO GRAND.
Sung by Mr. John Short, at Watchet.

There is no better known or more popular chantey than Rio Grand which is included in nearly every Collection. The tune varies but little.

No. 22. LUCY LONG.
Sung by Mr. John Short, at Watchet.

I know of no other printed version of this chantey. The chorus is curiously disjointed in its rhythm.

No. 23. THE BLACK BALL LINE.
Sung by Mr. John Short, at Watchet.

Mr. Robbins sang me another version of this chantey which is printed in the F.S.S. *Journal* (v. 37). See also Tozer (No. 7).

No. 24. FIRE ! FIRE !
Sung by Mr. John Short, at Watchet.

Tozer (No. 41) prints a variant of this as a pumping chantey, and I collected another very interesting form of it from Mr. Conway.

No. 25. A-ROVING.
Sung by Mr. John Short, at Watchet.

This, like Rio Grand, is well known to, and sung freely by sailors, and versions of it are to be found in all the best Collections. See also the F.S.S. *Journal* (ii, 245) and *The Scottish Students' Song Book* (p. 131).

No. 26. HEAVE AWAY, MY JOHNNY.
Sung by Mr. John Short, at Watchet.

See also Whall (p. 79) : *Music of the Waters* (p. 54) ; and *Folk Songs from Somerset* (No. 123).

No. 27. HAUL AWAY, JOE.
Sung by Mr. John Short, at Watchet.

Mr. Robbins sang me a mixolydian variant of this chantey which is printed (together with a dorian version quoted from Harper's *Magazine*) in F.S.S. *Journal*, v. p. 31. Tozer (No. 31), Bullen (No. 39), and Whall (p. 117) publish major versions of the tune. The air here printed is in the dorian mode. Mr. Short described it as a " tacks and sheets " chantey.

No. 28. SALLY BROWN.
Sung by Mr. Charles Robbins, at London.

Major versions are printed in *Music of the Waters* (p. 48), Whall (p. 64), Tozer (No. 1), Bradford and Fagge, and Bullen (No. 5). Tozer and Bullen give it as a capstan-chantey, but Mr. Robbins told me he always used it as a pulling-chantey.

The tune given here is a very curious one : both the third and sixth notes of the scale oscillate between major and minor.

No. 29. LOWLANDS LOW.
Sung by Mr. Richard Perkins, at St. Ives.

I do not know of any other variant of this beautiful chantey. The tune is in a six-note mode, the sixth degree of the scale being absent.

No. 30. SHALLOW BROWN.
Sung by Mr. John Short, at Watchet.

See also Tozer (No. 43), Whall (p. 119) and *Music of the Waters* (p. 48).

British ships, unlike American, always carried limejuice ; hence the British sailor was nicknamed " a limejuicer " by his American comrades.

No. 31. SING, SALLY O.
Sung by Mr. George Conway, at the Sailors' Home, London Dock.

The words are negro ; but the air, which is in the dorian mode, is a variant of " Haul Away, Joe " (No. 27). Bullen prints another version under the heading of " Mudder Dinah " (see Introduction, p. xvi).

No. 32. POOR OLD REUBEN RANZO.

Sung by Mr. John Short, at Watchet.

This chantey is a very generally known one, and versions of it are to be found in all the chief Collections. Who Reuben Ranzo was no one seems to know; Mr. Whall suggests that "Ranzo" may be a corruption of "Lorenzo."*

No. 33. GENERAL TAYLOR.

Sung by Mr. John Short, at Watchet.

I know of no other printed versions of this chantey, nor have I heard it sung by anybody else.

"General Taylor gained the day" refers no doubt to the victory which he gained over Santa Anna (see Note to No. 1).

The grace notes in the chorus are very remarkable and were beautifully sung by Mr. Short.

No. 34. OLD STORMEY.

Sung by Mr. John Short, at Watchet.

All the chief Collections print versions of this; neither words nor tune vary very much.

No. 35. BULLY IN THE ALLEY.

Sung by Mr. John Short, at Watchet.

I have no variants of this nor do I know of any printed version of it.

No. 36. LIZA LEE.

Sung by Mr. John Short, at Watchet.

The only variant of this that I know of is printed by Bullen (No. 27).

No. 37. HAUL ON THE BOWLINE.

Sung by Mr. John Short, at Watchet.

See also Tozer (No. 18), Bullen (No. 37), Bradford and Fagge (No. 1), and Miss Smith (p. 13).

No. 38. PADDY DOYLE.

Sung by Mr. John Short, at Watchet.

Versions of this are given by Bullen (No. 40), Tozer (No. 35) and Whall (p. 115).

This chantey seems always to have been used to accompany one particular operation, the bunting of a sail. This, if I understand it correctly, was

---

* It is possible that English chanteymen learned the name from Scandinavian sailors, for I am told that Danish sailors often sing about Daniel Rantzau (1529-69), who commanded the Danish forces in the seven-years (or three-crown) war with Sweden (1563-70).

the concluding and culminating act of the somewhat laborious process of furling, when the bunt, *i.e.* the middle folds of a half-furled sail, was raised on to the yard with one strong pull. The extra lines given in the text may be alternative versions used for the sake of variety; although, according to one of my informants, it was sometimes necessary to sing more than one verse. On his ship the second verse was always " We'll all throw dirt at the cook "; and when this was being chanted, the cook would come out of his galley, look up smilingly at the men on the yard, and on the conclusion of the song, wave his hat, laugh and retire.

No. 39. KNOCK A MAN DOWN.
Sung by Mr. John Short, at Watchet.

Whall (p. 93), Tozer (No. 22), Bullen (No. 32) Bradford and Fagge (No. 2), and Miss Smith (p. 18) all give versions of this chantey, which is usually known as " Blow the man down." I have supplemented Mr. Short's words—he could only remember two stanzas—with lines from other versions.

No. 40. JOHNNY BOWKER.
Sung by Mr. John Short, at Watchet.

This is included in all the well-known Collections. It is one of the single-pull chanteys, and is generally used for " bunting " a sail.

No. 41. TIDDY I O.
Sung by Mr. Rapsey, at Bridgwater.

In no other Collection that I know of is this chantey printed. I have noted no variants.

No. 42. ROUND THE CORNER, SALLY.
Sung by Mr. John Short, at Watchet.

I do not know of any printed version of this chantey, nor have I myself collected any variants.

No. 43. SO HANDY.
Sung by Mr. John Short, at Watchet.
See also Tozer (No. 30) and Whall (p. 128).

No. 44. A LONG TIME AGO.
Sung by Mr. James Tucker, at Bristol.

This is not included in any of the chief Collections, nor have I noted any variants.

No. 45. CHEERLY MAN.
Sung by Mr. John Short, at Watchet.

Whall (p. 111) and Miss Smith (p. 22) both give versions of this. Mr. Short told me this was the first chantey he learned and he thought it must have been the " first chantey ever invented."

No. 46. THE SAILOR LIKES HIS BOTTLE O.
Sung by Mr. John Short, at Watchet.

The only variant of this chantey, so far as I am aware, is one printed by Tozer (No. 29).

The tune is a close variant of " Gently Johnny my Jingalo " (*Folk Songs from Somerset*, No. 89).

No. 47. THE DEAD HORSE.
Sung by Mr. John Short, at Watchet.

See also Bullen (No. 29) and Tozer (No. 47).

This, although often used as a pulling-chantey, really forms part of a ceremony which was performed on board at the end of the first month at sea. It was customary for the first month's wages to be paid in advance before leaving port, the money being either spent by the men on shore or given to their wives and families. During the first month at sea, therefore, they were earning nothing, but merely paying off their indebtedness, *i.e.* working off the dead horse. The song was sung very slowly and solemnly round the ship, in procession, headed by a man carrying, or dragging at the end of a rope, an effigy of a horse made of canvas or the straw of an old bed. At the conclusion of the song the horse was triced to the foreyard, and then, in silence, cut away and dropped into the sea.

No. 48. WHISKY FOR MY JOHNNY.
Sung by Mr. James Tucker, at Bristol.

Versions of this chantey are printed in all the chief Collections. The words given in the text have been derived from different singers.

No. 49. BONNY WAS A WARRIOR.
Sung by Mr. John Short, at Watchet.

See also Bullen (No. 31), Tozer (No. 25) and Miss Smith (pp. 36 and 53)

Mr. Short sang " Bonny " not " Boney," which is the more usual pronunciation ; while his rendering of " John " was something between the French " Jean " and the English " John."

No. 50. BLOW, BOYS, COME BLOW TOGETHER.

Sung by Mr. John Short, at Watchet.

This is a well known chantey and is included in all the chief Collections.

No. 51. HANGING JOHNNY.

Sung by Mr. John Short, at Watchet.

In character the tune recalls "The Wearing of the Green." It is printed by Tozer (No. 28), Bullen (No. 24) and Whall (p. 130).

No. 52. A HUNDRED YEARS ON THE EASTERN SHORE.

Sung by Mr. John Short, at Watchet.

Tozer prints a variant (No. 34). I know of no other.

No. 53. SHANADAR.

SECOND VERSION

Sung by Mr. James Thomas, at Camborne.

This, a shortened form of No. 11, was one that Mr. Thomas often heard on " The City of Washington," in which ship he sailed to America in 1870.

No. 54. IN FRISCO BAY.

Sung by Captain Hole, at Watchet.

Captain Hole told me that this was often sung in the days when he was a midshipman in the Merchant Service. I do not know of any other printed version, nor have I collected any variants.

No. 55. SHALLOW BROWN.

SECOND VERSION.

Sung by Mr. Robert Ellison, at Belvedere, Woolwich.

This is not printed elsewhere. The words have a negro flavour.

No. 56. WON'T YOU GO MY WAY ?

Sung by Mr. John Short, at Watchet.

This is not, I believe, published elsewhere, nor have I collected any variants.

No. 57. WO STORMALONG.

Sung by Mr. Robert Ellison, at Belvedere, Woolwich.

I know of no other version of this chantey.

No. 58. O BILLY RILEY.

Sung by Mr. John Short, at Watchet.

I have no variants of this and I know of no other published version.

No. 59. TOM IS GONE TO HILO.

Sung by Mr. John Short, at Watchet.

This is printed by Tozer (No. 23), Bullen (No. 23), Whall (p. 74) and Miss Smith (p. 33).

No. 60. TOMMY'S GONE AWAY.

Sung by Mr. John Short, at Watchet.

This may be a variant of the preceding number, though the same singer sang them both. I cannot trace it anywhere else. Mr. Short said that this was used not only as a pulling chantey but also when they were screwing cotton into the hold at New Orleans